# DYSON ONTRAC
## Hands-On Review: Before you buy one

*A Comprehensive Guide to Cutting-Edge Audio Innovation and Performance*

**Alejandro S. Diego**

# Table of Contents

# Introduction

In a world where technology constantly pushes the boundaries of what we once thought possible, Dyson has always been at the forefront of innovation. Known for revolutionizing household appliances with their cutting-edge vacuum cleaners and air purifiers, Dyson has now set its sights on the audio industry. This leap into the realm of premium headphones has captivated the tech world, and the result is nothing short of spectacular: the Dyson OnTrac headphones.

Dyson's journey into the headphone market is a testament to their relentless pursuit of excellence and innovation. From their first groundbreaking vacuum cleaner to their sophisticated air purifiers, Dyson has consistently delivered products that redefine their respective categories. Their expertise in engineering and design has now been channeled into creating a pair of headphones that promise not only exceptional sound quality but also unparalleled comfort and advanced features.

The Dyson OnTrac headphones stand as a bold statement in the audio world. With their sleek design, customizable options, and impressive battery life, they are designed to meet the needs of even the most discerning audiophiles. These headphones boast up to 55 hours of battery life, ensuring that your music, podcasts, and calls can continue uninterrupted for days on end. This is a significant advantage over many competitors, making the OnTrac headphones a compelling choice for those who value longevity and reliability.

In the competitive landscape of high-end headphones, the Dyson OnTrac faces formidable rivals such as the AirPods Max and the Sonos Ace. Apple's AirPods Max have set a high bar with their impeccable sound quality and seamless integration with Apple's ecosystem. Similarly, the Sonos Ace is celebrated for its outstanding audio performance and versatile functionality. However, Dyson brings its own unique strengths to the table, offering a distinctive blend of innovation, sound quality, and user experience that sets the OnTrac headphones apart.

This book aims to provide a comprehensive guide to the Dyson OnTrac headphones, offering a detailed look at their design, features, and performance. We will explore how Dyson's latest creation compares with market leaders like the AirPods Max and Sonos Ace, delving into the intricacies of their engineering and the nuances of their user experience. Whether you are a tech enthusiast, an audiophile, or someone looking for the best headphones to suit your lifestyle, this book promises to equip you with all the insights you need.

Get ready to embark on a journey through the world of premium audio. As we uncover the secrets behind the Dyson OnTrac headphones, you will discover why these headphones are more than just a piece of technology—they are a testament to Dyson's commitment to innovation and excellence. Prepare to be amazed, informed, and inspired as we delve into everything you need to know about the Dyson OnTrac headphones.

# Dyson's Over-Engineering Approach

Dyson's over-engineering approach is evident in every facet of the OnTrac headphones, showcasing the company's dedication to pushing the boundaries of what personal audio devices can achieve. Known for their meticulous attention to detail and commitment to innovative design, Dyson has crafted a pair of headphones that are not only technologically advanced but also remarkably user-friendly.

One of the standout features of the Dyson OnTrac headphones is the integration of high-capacity lithium-ion battery cells directly into the headband. This ingenious design choice serves multiple purposes. First and foremost, it significantly extends the battery life, allowing for up to 55 hours of continuous use. This exceptional battery performance ensures that users can enjoy their music, podcasts, and calls without the constant need to recharge, making the OnTrac headphones ideal for long trips and extended listening sessions.

However, Dyson's integration of the batteries into the headband is not solely about extending battery life. It also plays a crucial role in the overall comfort of the headphones. By strategically placing the battery cells across the headband, Dyson has achieved a balanced weight distribution that enhances comfort during prolonged use. This thoughtful approach to weight dispersion prevents the headphones from feeling top-heavy or causing pressure points on the ears and head, a common issue with many high-end headphones.

The headband itself is designed with multiple cushioning points that evenly distribute the weight, reducing the strain on any single area. This careful consideration of ergonomics ensures that the headphones remain comfortable even during extended listening sessions. The cushioning materials are high-quality and breathable, preventing heat build-up and ensuring that the headband feels comfortable against the skin.

Dyson's commitment to over-engineering is also reflected in the build quality of the OnTrac headphones. Every component, from the headband to the ear cups, is crafted with precision and care. The materials used are not only durable but also luxurious, providing a premium feel that enhances the overall user experience. This attention to detail ensures that the headphones are not only functional but also aesthetically pleasing and built to last.

In summary, Dyson's over-engineering approach in the OnTrac headphones is a testament to their dedication to innovation and user satisfaction. The integration of high-capacity lithium-ion battery cells into the headband not only provides an impressive battery life but also enhances comfort through thoughtful weight dispersion. This combination of advanced technology and ergonomic design sets the Dyson OnTrac headphones apart from their competitors, offering a unique blend of performance, comfort, and style.

## Customization Options

One of the most compelling aspects of the Dyson OnTrac headphones is the extensive customization options available to users. Unlike many high-end headphones that offer a standard design, Dyson has introduced a level of personalization that allows users to make their headphones truly their own. This focus on customization not only enhances the aesthetic appeal but also reflects Dyson's commitment to user-centric design.

The ear cups and outer caps of the Dyson OnTrac headphones are fully customizable. This means you can easily switch out the ear cups and caps to match your style or mood. With a simple twist, the ear cups can be replaced with different colors, allowing for a wide range of color combinations. This feature is particularly appealing to users who enjoy changing up their look or who want their headphones to match their outfit or personal style. The ability to customize these components adds a layer of individuality that is rare in the headphone market.

The range of available color combinations further enhances the customization experience. Dyson offers a variety of colors for both the ear cups and outer caps, from classic blacks and whites to vibrant blues, reds, and more. This extensive palette ensures that there is a combination to suit every taste. Whether you prefer a sleek, professional look or a bold, eye-catching design, the Dyson OnTrac headphones can be tailored to meet your preferences.

Beyond customization, the Dyson OnTrac headphones are built with high-quality materials that ensure durability and a premium feel. The materials used in the construction of the headphones are selected for their robustness and comfort. The headband, for example, is made from a blend of lightweight yet sturdy materials that provide both flexibility and strength. The ear cups are cushioned with memory foam, which not only adds to the comfort but also helps in noise isolation, enhancing the overall listening experience.

The overall build quality of the Dyson OnTrac headphones is exceptional. Every component is meticulously crafted to ensure long-lasting performance. The headphones feel solid and well-constructed, exuding a sense of luxury that is often missing in other products. This attention to detail in both design and material selection means that the headphones can withstand daily wear and tear, making them a reliable choice for regular use.

Durability is a key factor in the design of the Dyson OnTrac headphones. The materials used are not only aesthetically pleasing but also resistant to scratches and minor impacts. This ensures that the headphones maintain their appearance and functionality over time. The robust construction is complemented by a high level of craftsmanship, with each pair undergoing rigorous quality control checks to meet Dyson's exacting standards.

In conclusion, the customization options available for the Dyson OnTrac headphones set them apart in the market. The ability to personalize the ear cups and outer caps with various color combinations allows users to express their individual style. Combined with the use of high-quality materials and exceptional build quality, these headphones offer a premium experience that is both durable and aesthetically pleasing. Dyson's attention to detail and commitment to user satisfaction is evident in every aspect of the OnTrac headphones, making them a standout choice for those seeking both performance and personalization.

# Comfort Level During Use

The Dyson OnTrac headphones excel in providing exceptional comfort, even during extended periods of use. This focus on comfort and usability sets them apart in the competitive landscape of high-end audio devices. When comparing the Dyson OnTrac to other headphones like the AirPods Max, several factors come into play that highlight Dyson's meticulous attention to detail in design and ergonomics.

One of the primary considerations for comfort is the weight of the headphones. The Dyson OnTrac headphones weigh 450 grams, which is slightly heavier than the AirPods Max at 385 grams. While this weight difference might initially seem negligible, it can have a significant impact on comfort during prolonged use. Dyson has addressed this potential issue by incorporating an advanced weight distribution system.

Dyson's approach to weight distribution involves strategically placing high-capacity lithium-ion battery cells within the headband. This design not only ensures long battery life but also helps to balance the weight of the headphones more evenly across the head. By distributing the weight away from the ear cups, Dyson reduces the pressure on the ears and head, which is often a source of discomfort with other headphones.

The headband itself is designed with multiple cushioning points that further enhance comfort. These cushioning points are made from high-quality, breathable materials that prevent heat buildup and ensure a soft, comfortable fit against the skin. The memory foam ear cups also contribute to the overall comfort by conforming to the shape of the ears, providing a snug yet gentle seal that enhances both comfort and noise isolation.

In terms of usability, the Dyson OnTrac headphones are designed to be user-friendly and practical for everyday use. The intuitive controls, such as the joystick on the right ear cup, allow for easy adjustments to volume, playback, and track selection without needing to fumble with a connected device. This ease of use is particularly beneficial during activities like commuting or working, where quick and effortless control is essential.

User comfort analysis indicates that Dyson's efforts in weight distribution and ergonomic design significantly improve the overall experience. Users report that despite the headphones' substantial weight, the balanced design prevents the usual discomfort associated with heavier headphones. This makes the Dyson OnTrac suitable for long listening sessions, whether you're on a long flight, working at your desk, or simply enjoying music at home.

Furthermore, the adjustable headband allows users to customize the fit to their liking, accommodating various head sizes and shapes. This adjustability ensures that the headphones remain securely in place without exerting excessive pressure, enhancing comfort over extended periods.

In comparison to the AirPods Max, the Dyson OnTrac offers a different approach to comfort. While the AirPods Max are lighter, their weight distribution is more concentrated around the ear cups, which can lead to fatigue over time. Dyson's innovative design spreads the weight more evenly, reducing this issue and providing a more comfortable fit for longer durations.

In summary, the Dyson OnTrac headphones are designed with a keen focus on comfort and usability, making them an excellent choice for extended use. The advanced weight distribution, high-quality cushioning materials, and ergonomic design ensure that users can enjoy their audio experience without discomfort. Whether you're a frequent traveler, a busy professional, or a dedicated audiophile, the Dyson OnTrac headphones offer a blend of comfort and performance that is hard to match.

## Advanced Features

The Dyson OnTrac headphones are packed with advanced features designed to enhance the listening experience and provide a seamless, intuitive user interface. These features, including on-head detection, real-time sound tracking, noise cancellation and transparency modes, and intuitive controls, set the OnTrac headphones apart from many competitors in the market.

One of the standout features is the on-head detection. This smart technology automatically pauses playback when you remove the headphones from your head and resumes when you put them back on. This functionality is particularly useful in daily life, where interruptions are common. It ensures that you never miss a beat, literally, and helps conserve battery life by stopping playback when the headphones are not in use.

Real-time sound tracking is another innovative feature of the Dyson OnTrac headphones. This technology continuously monitors both in-ear and external volume levels, providing live reports through the My Dyson app. This feature helps protect your hearing by alerting you to potentially harmful sound levels, allowing you to adjust the volume accordingly. The My Dyson app offers additional insights and controls, enabling you to fine-tune the listening experience to suit your preferences. You can monitor real-time sound exposure and receive personalized recommendations, making it a valuable tool for maintaining auditory health.

Noise cancellation and transparency modes are critical features for modern headphones, and Dyson has excelled in implementing these technologies in the OnTrac headphones. The noise cancellation feature effectively blocks out external noises, allowing you to immerse yourself fully in your music or calls. This is particularly beneficial in noisy environments, such as airplanes or busy offices. The transparency mode, activated with a simple double-tap on the ear cup, allows you to hear external sounds without removing the headphones. This is perfect for situations where you need to stay aware of your surroundings, such as when crossing the street or listening for announcements.

The performance of these modes is impressive, with users reporting that the noise cancellation rivals that of top-tier competitors. The seamless transition between noise cancellation and transparency mode ensures that you can easily switch between immersive listening and situational awareness without any hassle.

Intuitive controls further enhance the usability of the Dyson OnTrac headphones. The right ear cup features a joystick that allows for easy control of various functions. You can adjust the volume, skip tracks, play or pause music, and even activate Siri with a simple push or tilt of the joystick. This design eliminates the need to constantly reach for your connected device, making it convenient to manage your listening experience on the go. The joystick's placement and functionality are user-friendly, allowing for quick and effortless adjustments.

The integration with Siri adds another layer of convenience, enabling voice commands for hands-free control. Whether you need to make a call, send a message, or ask for directions, activating Siri through the headphones simplifies the process and keeps you connected without disrupting your activities.

In summary, the advanced features of the Dyson OnTrac headphones, including on-head detection, real-time sound tracking, noise cancellation and transparency modes, and intuitive controls, offer a comprehensive and user-centric listening experience. These features not only enhance the quality of sound but also provide practical benefits that make the headphones a versatile and valuable accessory for everyday use. Dyson's commitment to innovation and user convenience is evident in every aspect of the OnTrac headphones, making them a top choice for anyone seeking cutting-edge audio technology.

# Sound Quality

From the moment you put on the Dyson OnTrac headphones, the sound quality makes a strong impression. The audio is crisp, clear, and well-balanced across the frequency spectrum. The bass is deep and punchy without overwhelming the mids and highs, which remain clear and detailed. Whether you're listening to complex orchestral pieces or bass-heavy electronic music, the OnTrac headphones deliver a satisfying and immersive audio experience.

Comparing the Dyson OnTrac to its main competitors, such as the AirPods Max and Sonos Ace, reveals some interesting nuances. The AirPods Max, known for their impeccable sound quality, offer a slightly more refined audio experience, particularly in the mid and high frequencies. Apple's tuning ensures that vocals and instruments are rendered with stunning clarity, making them a favorite among audiophiles. The Sonos Ace, on the other hand, excels in providing a robust and versatile sound profile that works well across various genres. It delivers a balanced audio experience with a slight emphasis on the bass, which makes it enjoyable for casual listening and home use.

The Dyson OnTrac headphones hold their ground firmly in this competitive landscape. While they may not surpass the AirPods Max in sheer audio refinement, they come very close, providing a sound quality that will satisfy even discerning listeners. The bass is impactful without being overpowering, the mids are rich and full, and the highs are clear without being harsh. This balanced tuning makes the OnTrac suitable for a wide range of music genres, from classical to pop to rock.

A notable aspect of the Dyson OnTrac is the inclusion of EQ presets, which allow users to tailor the sound to their preferences. The available presets include Enhanced, Bass Boost, and Neutral. The Enhanced preset slightly boosts all frequencies, giving the music a more dynamic and lively feel.

The Bass Boost preset emphasizes the lower frequencies, adding depth and power to the bass, which is perfect for genres like hip-hop and EDM. The Neutral preset offers a flat response, providing a more natural and uncolored sound that is ideal for audiophiles and those who prefer an accurate representation of their music.

However, a significant drawback is the lack of customizable EQ settings. Unlike some competitors that allow users to fine-tune their audio experience by adjusting individual frequency bands, the Dyson OnTrac limits users to the three preset options. This limitation might be a dealbreaker for some audiophiles who enjoy tweaking their sound profile to match their exact preferences. The inability to create custom EQ profiles means that users must rely on the preset options, which, while good, may not satisfy everyone.

In terms of noise cancellation, the Dyson OnTrac performs admirably. The noise cancellation technology effectively reduces ambient noise, allowing users to focus on their music without distractions. This feature is particularly useful in noisy environments like public transport or busy offices. The transparency mode is equally impressive, letting in external sounds without compromising the audio quality. This mode is perfect for situations where you need to stay aware of your surroundings while enjoying your music.

In conclusion, the Dyson OnTrac headphones deliver impressive sound quality that competes well with top-tier models like the AirPods Max and Sonos Ace. While they may not offer the same level of audio refinement as the AirPods Max, they provide a balanced and enjoyable listening experience that will please a wide range of users. The inclusion of EQ presets adds some flexibility, though the lack of customizable EQ settings is a notable limitation. Overall, the Dyson OnTrac headphones offer a compelling blend of sound quality, advanced features, and user-friendly design that makes them a strong contender in the high-end headphone market.

## Battery Life and Charging

One of the most impressive features of the Dyson OnTrac headphones is their battery life. With up to 55 hours of continuous use on a single charge, these headphones significantly outperform many high-end competitors. This exceptional battery performance means you can enjoy your favorite music, podcasts, and calls for days on end without needing to recharge. Whether you're a frequent traveler, a busy professional, or simply someone who listens to audio throughout the day, the Dyson OnTrac headphones provide the reliability you need.

Comparing this to other high-end headphones, such as the AirPods Max and the Sonos Ace, the Dyson OnTrac clearly stands out. The AirPods Max offer up to 20 hours of battery life, which is impressive but still falls short of Dyson's offering. Similarly, the Sonos Ace, while delivering excellent sound quality and features, does not match the extended battery life of the OnTrac. This advantage makes the Dyson

OnTrac particularly appealing for users who prioritize long-lasting performance and minimal interruptions.

Charging the Dyson OnTrac headphones is both efficient and convenient, thanks to the inclusion of USB-C charging. USB-C is known for its fast charging capabilities and widespread compatibility, making it a practical choice for modern users. This ensures that you can quickly recharge your headphones and get back to enjoying your audio without lengthy downtime.

Another innovative feature is the ability to charge the headphones within their protective case. This hybrid case design not only protects the headphones when not in use but also serves as a charging station. This means you can recharge the headphones even when they're safely tucked away in your bag or on your desk. The case itself is a blend of hard shell and soft materials, providing robust protection while maintaining a sleek and portable form factor.

The hybrid case design offers both protection and usability. It is sturdy enough to safeguard the headphones from the bumps and knocks of daily life, yet compact enough to be easily carried around. The interior of the case is thoughtfully designed to hold the headphones securely, preventing any unnecessary movement that could cause damage. Additionally, the ability to charge the headphones while they are in the case adds an extra layer of convenience, allowing you to maintain battery life without having to unpack and repack the headphones every time they need a boost.

In summary, the Dyson OnTrac headphones excel in battery life and charging capabilities, offering up to 55 hours of use on a single charge. The use of USB-C for fast and efficient charging, combined with the innovative hybrid case design that allows for charging within the case, ensures that these headphones are always ready to go when you are. This focus on battery performance and user convenience makes the Dyson OnTrac a standout choice for those who value long-lasting, high-quality audio experiences.

# Day-to-Day Use

In the realm of day-to-day use, the Dyson OnTrac headphones truly excel. Their combination of advanced features, thoughtful design, and superior comfort makes them a reliable companion for various activities, whether you're at home, at work, or on the go.

Comfort is a crucial factor for headphones intended for extended use, and the Dyson OnTrac headphones deliver admirably in this regard. The generous padding on the ear cups and headband ensures a snug yet comfortable fit that doesn't become bothersome even after hours of continuous wear. The memory foam ear cups conform to the shape of your ears, providing a secure seal that enhances sound quality while remaining gentle on the skin. Reviewers have noted that despite the headphones' substantial weight, the excellent weight distribution across the headband mitigates any potential discomfort, allowing for prolonged use without fatigue.

Practical insights from users reveal that the intuitive controls add to the seamless user experience. The joystick on the right ear cup is particularly praised for its ease of use, allowing for quick adjustments to volume, playback, and track selection without needing to fumble with your connected device. This hands-on control is especially beneficial in situations where you need to make swift changes, such as during a workout or while commuting.

When it comes to travel and portability, the Dyson OnTrac headphones prove to be a versatile option. The sturdy yet compact hybrid case design protects the headphones from the rigors of travel, ensuring they remain in pristine condition no matter where you take them. The ability to charge the headphones within the case is a significant advantage for travelers, as it allows for convenient recharging without needing to remove the headphones from their protective shell. This feature, combined with the impressive battery life, means you can rely on the headphones throughout long journeys without worrying about running out of power.

Portability considerations extend beyond just the case. The headphones themselves are designed to be foldable, making them easy to pack into a bag or carry-on. Their robust construction ensures that they can withstand the occasional jostling and pressure that comes with travel, while their sleek design means they won't take up excessive space. Additionally, the customizable ear cups and outer caps provide a touch of personal flair, making your headphones not only functional but also stylish accessories.

In daily commutes or business trips, the noise cancellation feature becomes invaluable. It effectively blocks out the ambient noise of bustling city streets or the constant hum of an airplane cabin, allowing you to immerse yourself fully in your music or work without distractions. The transparency mode is equally useful, enabling you to remain aware of your surroundings when necessary, such as when navigating busy terminals or listening for announcements.

Overall, the Dyson OnTrac headphones excel in both comfort and usability over long periods, making them a practical choice for daily use. Their suitability for travel and portability considerations further enhance their appeal, ensuring they are ready to accompany you wherever you go. Whether you're a frequent traveler or someone who simply enjoys high-quality audio throughout the day, the Dyson OnTrac headphones offer a compelling combination of features that cater to your needs.

# Strengths, Weaknesses and Personal Recommendation

The Dyson OnTrac headphones bring a wealth of features and innovations to the table, making them a compelling choice in the competitive world of high-end audio equipment. Here's a summary of their strengths and weaknesses, a detailed comparison with notable alternatives like the Sonos Ace and AirPods Max, and some personal recommendations on who would benefit most from these headphones.

The Dyson OnTrac headphones offer an impressive array of strengths. One of the most notable is their exceptional battery life, providing up to 55 hours of continuous use. This feature alone sets them apart from many competitors, ensuring that users can enjoy extended listening sessions without frequent recharging. The integration of high-capacity lithium-ion battery cells into the headband not only contributes to this long battery life but also helps in evenly distributing the weight of the headphones, enhancing overall comfort.

Another strength is the customization options available. Users can personalize their headphones with interchangeable ear cups and outer caps, choosing from a variety of color combinations. This level of customization is rare in the headphone market and adds a unique, personal touch to the user experience. Additionally, the build quality is exceptional, with high-quality materials ensuring durability and a premium feel.

The advanced features of the Dyson OnTrac headphones are also worth noting. On-head detection, real-time sound tracking, effective noise cancellation, and intuitive joystick controls make these headphones both user-friendly and technologically advanced. These features enhance the listening experience by providing convenience and superior sound quality.

However, the Dyson OnTrac headphones are not without their drawbacks. The most significant is their weight. At 450 grams, they are heavier than many alternatives, including the AirPods Max, which can lead to discomfort during prolonged use. Despite Dyson's efforts to distribute the weight evenly, some users might still find them a bit cumbersome. Another notable limitation is the lack of customizable EQ settings. While the headphones offer preset EQ options such as Enhanced, Bass Boost, and Neutral, the inability to create personalized sound profiles might be a dealbreaker for audiophiles who enjoy tweaking their audio settings to perfection.

When comparing the Dyson OnTrac to the Sonos Ace and AirPods Max, several key points emerge. The AirPods Max are renowned for their impeccable sound quality and seamless integration with Apple devices. They offer a more refined audio experience, particularly in the mid and high frequencies, making them a favorite among audiophiles. The Sonos Ace, on the other hand, excels in providing a robust and versatile sound profile that works well across various genres. It delivers a balanced audio experience with a slight emphasis on the bass, which makes it enjoyable for casual listening and home use. However, both alternatives fall short in battery life when compared to the Dyson OnTrac, which remains one of the most significant advantages of Dyson's offering.

Considering these factors, the Dyson OnTrac headphones are best suited for users who prioritize battery life, innovative features, and customization. They are an excellent choice for frequent travelers who need long-lasting performance and for those who appreciate the ability to personalize their headphones. The advanced features like on-head detection, real-time sound tracking, and intuitive controls add significant value and convenience, making them a strong contender in the premium headphone market.

In conclusion, the Dyson OnTrac headphones represent a significant achievement in the realm of personal audio. Dyson's approach to blending advanced technology with practical design elements has resulted in a product that not only delivers on its promises but also sets new standards in several areas. The combination of long battery life, customization options, and advanced features makes these headphones an excellent choice for a wide range of users.

**Best Use Cases for Dyson OnTrac:**

- **Frequent Travelers:** The long battery life and ability to charge within the case make them perfect for long journeys.
- **Tech Enthusiasts:** Those who appreciate cutting-edge technology and advanced features will find much to love.
- **Customization Lovers:** If you enjoy personalizing your gear, the customizable ear cups and outer caps offer a unique appeal.

- **Music Aficionados:** While the lack of customizable EQ is a drawback, the overall sound quality and noise cancellation capabilities still make these headphones a great choice for enjoying music in various environments.

## Who Should Buy These Headphones?

- **Frequent Travelers:** The long battery life and travel-friendly features make them ideal for those always on the go.
- **Tech Enthusiasts:** Individuals who love exploring new and advanced technology will appreciate the innovative features of the Dyson OnTrac.
- **Style-Conscious Users:** Those who value customization and personal style will enjoy the customizable ear cups and outer caps.
- **Audiophiles:** Despite the lack of customizable EQ, the sound quality is still top-notch, making it a good choice for those who appreciate high-quality audio.

In summary, the Dyson OnTrac headphones offer a blend of innovation, performance, and personalization that is hard to match. They are a solid choice for anyone looking for high-quality, feature-rich headphones that can deliver a superior listening experience over extended periods. Whether you're a frequent traveler, a tech enthusiast, or someone who values both form and function, the Dyson OnTrac headphones are an excellent investment.

# Conclusion

As we conclude our exploration of the Dyson OnTrac headphones, it's clear that Dyson has brought its renowned expertise and innovative spirit to the world of high-end audio. Throughout this book, we've delved into the myriad features and design choices that make the OnTrac headphones a standout in the competitive landscape of premium headphones.

To recap, the Dyson OnTrac headphones offer an impressive battery life of up to 55 hours, far surpassing many competitors and ensuring long-lasting performance for users. The high-capacity lithium-ion battery cells integrated into the headband not only contribute to this longevity but also help distribute the weight more evenly, enhancing comfort during extended use. Customization options, including interchangeable ear cups and outer caps, allow users to personalize their headphones to suit their style, while high-quality materials and exceptional build quality ensure durability and a premium feel.

Advanced features such as on-head detection, real-time sound tracking, effective noise cancellation, and intuitive joystick controls enhance the user experience, making the headphones both user-friendly and technologically advanced. However, the headphones are not without their drawbacks. Their substantial weight might be a concern for some users, and the lack of customizable EQ settings could disappoint audiophiles who prefer to fine-tune their audio experience.

In comparison to other high-end headphones like the AirPods Max and Sonos Ace, the Dyson OnTrac holds its ground admirably. While the AirPods Max offer slightly more refined sound quality and the Sonos Ace excels in versatility, the Dyson OnTrac's exceptional battery life and innovative features provide a unique and compelling alternative.

The key takeaways from this book highlight the strengths and weaknesses of the Dyson OnTrac headphones, providing a comprehensive understanding of their capabilities and suitability for various users. The exceptional battery life, advanced features, and customization options make them an excellent choice for frequent travelers, tech enthusiasts, and style-conscious users. Despite some limitations, the overall performance and user experience offered by the Dyson OnTrac headphones are impressive.

In my final opinion, the Dyson OnTrac headphones represent a significant achievement in personal audio. Dyson's commitment to innovation and user satisfaction is evident in every aspect of the design and functionality of these headphones. They offer a blend of advanced technology, comfort, and personalization that is hard to match, making them a worthy investment for anyone seeking high-quality, long-lasting headphones.

As we wrap up this journey, I encourage you, the reader, to share your thoughts and experiences with the Dyson OnTrac headphones. Your insights and feedback are invaluable, helping others make informed decisions and allowing us all to appreciate the nuances of these remarkable devices. Engaging in conversations and sharing experiences enriches our understanding and enjoyment of these cutting-edge technologies. Let's continue the dialogue and explore the world of innovative audio together.

Thank you for joining me on this exploration of the Dyson OnTrac headphones. I hope this book has provided you with the information and insights you need to make an informed decision. Enjoy your listening experience, and don't hesitate to share your journey with others.

www.ingramcontent.com/pod-product-compliance
Lightning Source LLC
LaVergne TN
LVHW051624050326
832903LV00033B/4656